Photographs supplied by Empics Ltd

This publication has been prepared without the involvement of any recognised
Football Association, including the Scottish Football Association,
the Football Association of England or any companies and football players
whose names or images may appear in this book.

The information given in this book, including dates of matches, was correct
at the time of publication but may be subject to change.

THE UNOFFICIAL GUIDE TO

WORLD CUP 98

David Prole

Ladybird

The World Cup was first suggested by two French football officials, Henri Delaunay and Jules Rimet. It began in 1930 with only 13 competing nations, but has grown and grown until the competition now takes a busy month to complete.

In the 68 years since it was first started, only six nations have won the trophy. Uruguay have won twice, but did not qualify this year. But any one of the other five – Brazil (4 times), Germany and Italy (3 each), Argentina (twice) and England (once) – seems to have a reasonable chance of winning it again this time.

Brazil, with their free-flowing style and seemingly endless supply of great players, have the best record of any nation. Argentina have had some of the brightest stars, but are not as consistent as their rival South Americans.

Italy, wonderfully talented, and Germany, wonderfully organised, have led the European challenge. But England's fans will be hoping that the days of 1966, when Sir Alf Ramsey's team topped the world, can happen again under Glenn Hoddle.

Whatever happens, France 98 promises to give many happy footballing memories.

4

1934

ITALY TAKE OVER

1930

1938

URUGUAY IN LUCK

ITALY AGAIN

Like Uruguay, Italy won the tournament in their own country, beating Czechoslovakia 2–1 in extra time. Uruguay, who were still upset with European teams for not competing in 1930, refused to take part.

FIFA allowed Uruguay to stage the first World Cup, to mark 100 years of its existence. They were angry when only four European teams made the long sea journey to take part. Only 18 matches took place, with Uruguay beating Argentina 4–2 in the Final.

Although there were only two players left of the 1934 team, Italy were worthy winners, beating Hungary 4–2 in the Final in Paris. But they had been lucky in the semi-final, when Brazil rested Leonidas, who had scored eight goals in the competition. They had wanted to keep him fresh for the Final, but without him they lost 2–1 to Italy.

1950

1958

1954

URUGUAY SURPRISE

Uruguay won for the second time. This was the only World Cup to have a four-nation final play-off instead of a knockout. Brazil, the favourites, were beaten 2 – 1 by the Uruguayans in the deciding game. The match was watched by a record crowd of 199,000.

SO SAD, HUNGARY

PELE IN ACTION

Pele, aged only 17, started the competition as a reserve for the Brazil squad, but forced his way into the team. He and Vava both scored two goals in the Final, a 5 – 2 defeat of the host nation, Sweden.

IV CAMPEONATO
MUNDIAL DE
FUTEBOL
·TAÇA JULES RIMET·

JUNHO DE 1950
BRASIL

SUÈDE · SWEDEN · SUECIA · SCHWEDEN 8–29.6.19

FOOTBALL
FUTBOL
FUSSBALL

Hungary had not been beaten for almost four years, then lost to West Germany in the Final. They had been two goals up, but were beaten 3 – 2. In a festival of attacking football, each game averaged almost 5.5 goals.

England's Bobby Moore raises the World Cup

1966

1962

ALF'S TRIUMPH

1970

BRAZIL ONCE MORE

England were lucky to play all six matches at Wembley. They drew their first game with Uruguay, then won five in a row, against Mexico, France, Argentina, Portugal and West Germany, whom they beat 4–2 in the Final. The Queen rewarded England's manager for his team's success by making him a knight– Sir Alf Ramsey.

BRAZIL TREBLE

PEONATO MUNDIAL DE FUTBOL
LD FOOTBALL CHAMPIONSHIP
MPIONNAT MONDIAL DE FOOTBALL
CHILE 1962

Eight of the 1958 teams played again in 1962. Brazil kept the trophy, with a 3–1 win over Czechoslovakia in the Final, played in Santiago, Chile. The competition was affected by many examples of unfair play.

MEXICO 70
IX football world championship

Pele was as good as ever in his fourth World Cup. His opening goal put Brazil on their way to a 4–1 win in the Final in boiling-hot Mexico. Unlucky Italy, their opponents, were still weary from a 4–3 extra-time semi-final with West Germany.

WORLD CUP

JULY 11 to 1966 ENGLAND

(Sir Alf Ramsey)

7

1974

GERMANS HOLD ON

The Netherlands, the best team, did not win. In the Final they scored from a first-minute penalty, but were too sure of success and in the end they were beaten 2–1 by West Germany, who were playing on their home ground in Munich.

1978

AT LAST, ARGENTINA

After a long history of unexpected defeats, Argentina at last won the trophy. They beat The Netherlands 3–1 after extra time in a bad-tempered match that ended with amazing scenes of delight in their capital city, Buenos Aires.

1982

ROSSI TO THE RESCUE

Striker Paolo Rossi was in marvellous form throughout the competition. Italy owed most of their success to him. West Germany, who were upset by arguments among their players, reached the Final, but were well beaten, 3–1.

Winning captain Passarella, in 1978

1990

ITALIA 90

1986

ARGENTINA IN DISGRACE

A poor tournament, with far too much defensive play. The Final was like many of the other games, with hardly a shot at goal. Argentina had two men sent off and West Germany won by the only goal, a late penalty.

THE HAND OF GOD

England were confident and playing well in their quarter-final against Argentina when Diego Maradona scored a goal with his hand. Argentina went on to take the trophy, beating West Germany 3 – 2 in the Final.

1994

ITALY SHOT OUT

A generally happy competition, well staged by the United States. But again it was spoilt by a dull Final, decided when Roberto Baggio missed in a penalty shoot-out. That was not a proper way for Brazil to gain their fourth World Cup, nor a proper way for Italy to lose.

Maradona

Baggio's missed penalty

9

▶ He was born on 25 December 1944 – but for him Christmas came in June 1970 when he scored in all six of Brazil's matches in the World Cup finals

JAIRZINHO
(Brazil)

FRANZ BECKENBAUER
(West Germany)

▲ The first man to win the World Cup as captain (1974) and manager (1990)

EUSEBIO
(Portugal)

▼ Top scorer in 1966 with nine goals – and Portugal's greatest-ever player

JUST FONTAINE
(France)

▼ Scored 13 goals from six games in the 1958 World Cup finals – a record that seems unlikely to be beaten

10

DINO ZOFF
(Italy)

▶ **Goalkeeper for Italy in 112 international matches.** He followed another Juventus keeper, Gianpiero Combi, in captaining his country to a World Cup victory

LUISITO MONTI
(Argentina/Italy)

He was captain of Argentina in 1930 when they lost the first World Cup Final. Four years later, having changed his nationality, he helped Italy win the second

Pele
(Brazil)

▼ **Perhaps the greatest player ever.** He appeared in four World Cups, winning and scoring in 1958 (when still only 17 years old) and 1970

ROGER MILLA
(Cameroon)

▶ **The first African footballer to make an impact on the World Cup** – with appearances in 1982 and 1990. He spent most of his career with French clubs

GEOFF HURST
(England)

▶ **The only player to score three goals in a World Cup Final** (against West Germany in 1966)

11

PAOLO ROSSI
(Italy)

▼ **Scored three goals in the quarter-final,** two in the semi-final and one in the Final to win the 1982 trophy almost single-handedly

GERD MULLER
(West Germany)

▲ **Scored the winning goal in the 1974 Final –** his 68th and last goal for West Germany

FERENC PUSKAS
(Hungary)

▼ **Scorer of 83 goals in 84 matches.** His equaliser against West Germany in the 1954 Final was ruled offside and his team lost for the first time in nearly four years

GARY LINEKER
(England)

◄ **England's record goal scorer in the World Cup,** with ten from two tournaments (1986 and 1990)

KENNY DALGLISH
(Scotland)

► **Winner of almost 30 medals from major competitions as player and manager.** He appeared in three World Cup finals

12

BOBBY MOORE
(England)

▶ **The only English captain to lift the World Cup,** and one of his country's greatest players

ROBERTO BAGGIO
(Italy)

▲ **A World and European Player of the Year,** but he is sadly remembered for his missed penalty in the 1994 Final shoot-out

BOBBY CHARLTON
(England)

▶ **Played in three World Cups and was outstanding in the 1966 victory,** setting England on their way with a marvellous goal against Mexico

MARADONA
(Argentina)

▼ **Winner and Player of the Tournament in 1986,** a losing finalist in 1990

UWE SEELER
(West Germany)

◀ **Scored 43 goals in 73 international matches.** Seeler (in white) and Pele are the only two men to score in four World Cup finals

AUSTRIA

Previous appearances:
1934 (4th), 1954 (3rd), 1958, 1978, 1982, 1990
Manager: Herbert Prohaska
Players to watch: Konsel, Polster, Feiersinger
Qualification: Top of European Group 4

Coach Prohaska deserves praise for the way in which he has taken charge of a poor team and helped them to a place among Europe's best. They let in only four goals in ten qualifying matches.

BELGIUM

Previous appearances:
1930, 1934, 1938, 1954, 1970, 1982, 1986 (4th), 1990, 1994
Manager: Georges Leekens
Players to watch: Scifo, Oliveira, De Wilde, Nilis
Qualification: 2nd in European Group 7, then play-off

The Belgians often fail to do as well as they should. On paper, they have had some fine teams. In action, they rarely do as well as their fans expect.

BULGARIA

Previous appearances: 1962, 1966, 1970, 1974, 1986, 1994 (4th)
Manager: Hristo Bonev
Players to watch: Stoichkov, Letchkov, Ivanov
Qualification: Top of European Group 5

The Bulgarians had not won any of their 16 World Cup matches before 1994. Then they surprised the world by reaching the semi-finals. Several of that team remain and coach Bonev's well-drilled squad will be hard to defeat.

14

CROATIA

Previous appearances: None
Manager: Miroslav Blazevic
Players to watch: Suker, Boban, Boksic, Stimac
Qualification: 2nd in European Group 1, then play-off

Davor Suker

Croatian players love to play attacking football. They made many friends in England when reaching the quarter-finals of the European Championship in 1996. Same again this time, perhaps?

DENMARK

Previous appearance: 1986
Manager: Bo Johansson
Players to watch: Schmeichel, B Laudrup, M Laudrup
Qualification: Top of European Group 1

Peter Schmeichel

Few small countries have done as well as Denmark in recent years, but many of their top players are no longer young. They had to fight hard to get through their qualifying group, and look unlikely to do very well in France.

15

AM TALK • TEAM TALK • TEAM TALK • TEAM TALK • TI

ENGLAND

Paul Ince

Previous appearances: 1950, 1954, 1958, 1962, 1966 (winners), 1970, 1982, 1986, 1990 (4th)
Manager: Glenn Hoddle
Players to watch: Shearer, Seaman, Beckham, Ince
Qualification: Top of European Group 2

England's performance in France could well depend on one man – their main striker, **Alan Shearer.** In 1996 he became the world's most expensive player when he transferred from Blackburn to Newcastle for £15 million (a record which has since been beaten). English fans will be hoping he has fully recovered from the injury which kept him out of the early months of this season. England are well organised in defence, with Seaman an outstanding keeper, and will be very hard to beat. Whether they have the all-round talent to defeat the world's best is not so certain.

Glenn Hoddle

FRANCE

Previous appearances:
1930, 1934, 1938, 1954,
1958 (3rd), 1966, 1978,
1982 (4th), 1986 (3rd)
Manager: Aime Jacquet
Players to watch:
Zidane, Karembeu, Ba,
Djorkaeff
Qualification: Host nation

Youri Djorkaeff

Ibrahim Ba

Christian Karembeu

The French often lose top players to other countries, but keep on finding more. Ibrahim Ba is a typical example of the youngsters coming through, and they often are able to play in various positions. Only five nations have won the World Cup in their own countries. France aim to make it six.

17

GERMANY

Previous appearances:
1934 (3rd), 1938, 1954 (winners)
1958 (4th), 1962, 1966 (2nd),
1970 (3rd), 1974 (winners),
1978, 1982 (2nd), 1986 (2nd),
1990 (winners), 1994
Manager: Hubert "Berti" Vogts
Players to watch:
Kohler, Klinsmann,
Bierhoff, Sammer
Qualification: Top of
European Group 9

They have the best World Cup record after Brazil, but they nearly did not qualify this time. Only a last-minute goal in their final match, against the bottom nation, Albania, took them through. The Germans usually get better as a tournament goes on, which is one reason why they reach so many finals. No team will be better prepared.

Oliver Bierhoff

ITALY

Previous appearances: 1934 (winners), 1938 (winners), 1950, 1954, 1962, 1966, 1970 (2nd), 1974, 1978 (4th), 1982 (winners), 1986, 1990 (3rd), 1994 (2nd)
Coach: Cesare Maldini
Players to watch: Paolo Maldini, Del Piero, Zola, Albertini
Qualification: 2nd in European Group 2, then play-off.

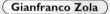

Gianfranco Zola

One of the favourites to win the tournament, although they only just qualified in the play-offs after being second to England in their group. They have so many good players that they should have a very good chance, but they will need to play more like a team and less like a collection of single stars

NETHERLANDS

Jaap Stam

Patrick Kluivert

Previous appearances:
1934, 1938, 1974 (2nd),
1978 (2nd), 1990, 1994
Manager: Guus Hiddink
Players to watch: Bergkamp,
Kluivert, Stam, Jonk
Qualification: Top of European
Group 7

he Netherlands are
still trying to
recapture the great
days of the 1970s and 80s,
when Cruyff, Neeskens,
Gullit, Rijkaard and Van Basten were
among the world's greatest players.
The Dutch only just qualified this time, after
losing to third-placed Turkey. Yet they had
one of the best goal records of any nation –
26 scored and only four let in.

NORWAY

Previous appearances: 1938, 1994
Manager: Egil Olsen
Players to watch: Leonhardsen, Flo, Rekdal
Qualification: Top of European Group 3

Kjetil Rekdal

Norway did badly in the 1994 World Cup, but have a much stronger squad now. They let in only two goals in eight qualifying games and so will not lack confidence. They might even manage to pull off a surprise or two.

ROMANIA

Previous appearances: 1930, 1934, 1938, 1970, 1990, 1994
Manager: Anghel Iordanescu
Players to watch: Hagi, Popescu, Petrescu, Stelea
Qualification: Top of European Group 8

The Romanians have improved a lot in recent years. They reached the last eight in the 1994 World Cup, and qualified this time with almost a year to spare.

Gheorghe Hagi

SCOTLAND

Gary McAllister

Previous appearances: 1954, 1958, 1974, 1978, 1982, 1986, 1990
Manager: Craig Brown
Players to watch: McAllister, Gallacher, Collins
Qualification: Best second-placed European team

John Collins

Craig Brown

Scotland have never got beyond the first stage of any World Cup finals. They are always well-motivated and give 100% effort for their loyal fans, who will be hoping that this is the year when their unwanted record comes to an end.

21

SPAIN

Previous appearances: 1934, 1950 (4th), 1962, 1966, 1978, 1982, 1986, 1990, 1994
Manager: Javier Clemente
Players to watch: Hierro, Guerrero, Raul, Zubizaretta
Qualification: Top of European Group 6

Raul

Coach Clemente has built and kept one of Europe's best teams. Most have played together for several seasons, and they are joined by a promising young striker, Raul. They will be among the most attractive teams to watch, and among the hardest to beat.

YUGOSLAVIA

Previous appearances: 1930 (semi-final), 1950, 1954, 1958, 1962, 1974, 1982, 1990
Manager: Slobodan Santrac
Players to watch: Stojkovic, Savicevic, Mijatovic, Jugovic
Qualification: 2nd in European Group 6, then play-off

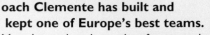

Dejan Savicevic

Civil war between various parts of the country does not seem to have affected the performance of Yugoslav footballers. They still keep coming along in big numbers and have a lot of talent. With luck, they could go a long way. A place in the last eight looks likely.

CAMEROON

Previous appearances: 1982, 1990, 1994
Manager: Jean-Manga Onguene
Players to watch: Song'o, Mboma, Etame
Qualification: Top of African Group 4

Spectacular goalkeeper and captain Song'o may be the busiest player in the Cameroon team. They do not look as strong as in 1990.

MOROCCO

Previous appearances: 1970, 1986, 1994
Manager: Henri Michel
Players to watch: Bassir, Nabet, El Hadji
Qualification: Top of African Group 5

Morocco were the highest scorers among the five African qualifiers. Their players have a lot of experience with European clubs and can be expected to do well.

NIGERIA

Previous appearance: 1994
Manager: Bora Milutinovic
Players to watch: Kanu, Babayaro, Oliseh
Qualification: Top of African Group 1

The team known as *Super Eagles* qualified easily.
Now they have to show if they can match the big boys. A lot depends on Nwankwo Kanu of Inter Milan, who had heart surgery last year.

☪ TUNISIA

Previous appearance: 1978
Manager: Henry Kasperczak
Players to watch: Thabet, Beya, Sellimi
Qualification: Top of African Group 2

Janik Thabet

Tunisia were the first African nation to win a match at the World Cup finals, in 1978. They will be happy to do the same this time – their star player Rekhissa died while playing in a club game last year.

▶ SOUTH AFRICA

Previous appearances: None
Manager: Philippe Troussier
Players to watch: Masinga, Radebe, Fish

Qualification: Top of African Group 3

Lucas Radebe

South Africa will be hoping that their football team can match the achievement of their rugby union colleagues and win the World Cup. Being out of the competition for over 30 years has left them short of international experience, but *Bafana Bafana* (Zulu for 'The Boys') have players from top European clubs to boost their chances of success. A recent change of coach might be a gamble that pays off.

24

MEXICO

Previous appearances:
1930, 1950, 1954, 1958, 1962, 1966, 1970, 1978, 1986, 1994
Manager: Manuel Lapuente
Players to watch: Hermosillo, Galindo, Zague
Qualification: 1st in CONCACAF Group

Mexicans play almost all the year round. Having reached the finals yet again, they may be too tired to show their best form, despite their talent.

JAMAICA

Previous appearances: None
Manager: Rene Simoes
Players to watch: Burton, Hall, Goodison
Qualification: 3rd in CONCACAF Group

The *Reggae Boyz* seemed unlikely to qualify when they made a poor start. Then they suddenly hit form and earned a place in France, although they scored only seven times in ten matches. The event was rewarded by the granting of a public holiday.

USA

Previous appearances:
1930 (semi-final), 1934, 1950, 1990, 1994
Manager: Steve Sampson
Players to watch: Keller, Pope, Wynalda
Qualification: 2nd in CONCACAF Group

Few Americans play soccer for a living, but those who do are continuing to improve. The members of the national squad are scattered worldwide, all longing for another chance to show how they can do against the rest of the world.

ARGENTINA

Previous appearances:
1930 (2nd), 1934, 1958, 196
1966, 1974, 1978 (winners), 1982,
1986 (winners), 1990 (2nd), 1994
Manager: Daniel Passarella
Players to watch: Ortega,
Batistuta, Veron, Crespo
Qualification: Top in
South American Group

Ariel Ortega

Argentina have some fine youngsters, including
Ariel Ortega, who plays for Valencia in Spain.
Coach Passarella, who captained the winning team in
1978, will be looking to Italian-based players Batistuta,
Crespo and Veron
for most of his
team's goals.

BRAZIL

Denilson

Previous appearances:
The only country to play in all 15
World Cup tournaments. Winners
1958, 1962, 1970 and 1994; 2nd 1950;
3rd 1938, 1978; 4th 1974
Manager: Mario Zagallo
Players to watch: Ronaldo, Rivaldo,
Denilson, Roberto Carlos
Qualification: Holders

This nation produces
an amazing number
of star players. If all
their team are on form
at once, surely no other
country can stop them
from keeping the World Cup

by winning it for the fifth time. They look sure to score
more often than any other nation.

CHILE

Previous appearances:
1930, 1950, 1962 (3rd), 1966, 1974, 1982
Manager: Nelson Acosta
Players to watch: Zamorano, Salas, Tapia
Qualification: 4th in South American Group

Chile did surprisingly poorly in the qualifying group and got through only on goal difference. The Chileans seem unlikely to get as far as the second round.

COLOMBIA

Previous appearances: 1962, 1990, 1994
Manager: Hernan Dario Gomez
Players to watch: Valderrama, Rincon, Cabrera
Qualification: 3rd in South American Group

Valderrama is easy to spot because of his hairstyle, but he can play as well as pose. So can many others in a talented squad. But can they do as well in France as they do at home?

PARAGUAY

Previous appearances:
1930, 1950, 1958, 1986
Manager: Paulo Cesar Carpeggiani
Players to watch: Chilavert, Gamarra, Riverola
Qualification: 2nd in South American Group

The surprise success of the South American tournament. They have a goalkeeper likely to be a big name in the World Cup – Jose Luis Chilavert. He takes both penalties and free-kicks!

IRAN

Previous appearance: 1978
Manager: Tomislav Ivic
Players to watch: Ali Daei, Bagherl, Mansourian, Khakpur
Qualification: 4th in Asian Group, then play-off with Australia (1st in Oceania)

Iran have several high-quality players, but not all the squad are of that standard. Overall, they seem unlikely to match the top Europeans or South Americans, except in fighting spirit. They came from 0–2 to win the play-off in Australia.

Mohammed Khakpur

JAPAN

Previous appearances: None
Manager: Takeshi Okada
Players to watch: Miura, Nakata, Nanami
Qualification: 2nd in Asian Group B, then play-off with Iran

Football has grown at remarkable speed in Japan. From virtually nothing a few years ago, the country is in the World Cup for the first time, and the team could well cause a few surprises.

SAUDI ARABIA

Previous appearance: 1994
Manager: Carlos Alberto Parreira
Players to watch: Mehalel, Al-Jaber, Al-Shahrani
Qualification: 1st in Asian Group A

The Saudis reached the second round in 1994, on their first appearance in the competition. They will do well to repeat that success, because they appear to have made little improvement despite often changing their coach.

Sami Al-Jaber

SOUTH KOREA

Previous appearances: 1954, 1986, 1990, 1994
Manager: Cha Bum Kun
Players to watch: Myong-Bo, Yong-Soo, Min-Sung
Qualification: 1st in Asian Group B

The Korean players are very strong and quick. They are also very well organised, too, though they are short of tactical knowledge.

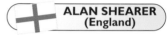

JURGEN KOHLER
(Germany)

◀ **One of the world's top defenders.** A key player when his club won last season's European Cup.

ALAN SHEARER
(England)

▶ **A regular scorer, twice transferred for the British record sum.** His full recovery from injury is vital to England's hopes.

ZINEDINE ZIDANE
(France)

◀ **One of the home team's many all-round players.** Could he be lucky? His 26th birthday falls in World Cup Final week.

JURGEN KLINSMANN
(Germany)

◀ **His second birthday was on the day England won the World Cup.** He is now determined to end his career by doing the same.

RONALDO
(Brazil)

▼ **Although only 22, he has already played with top clubs in Italy, Netherlands, Spain and Brazil.** Fabulously wealthy, he is known as the *King of Soccer*.

▶ **A long-serving goalkeeper who has never played better.** He was outstanding in the qualifying series.

MICHAEL KONSEL
(Austria)

31

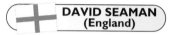

TRIFON IVANOV
(Bulgaria)

▶ **A strong, experienced defender and a never-give-up-captain.** He scored the winner in the vital qualifying game against Russia.

DAVID SEAMAN
(England)

▼ **After a long struggle, he has finally established himself as England's top goalkeeper.** He is one of the world's best, too.

ROBERTO CARLOS
(Brazil)

▼ **Plays left-back, but he is a versatile player who scores a high number of goals for a defender.** Watch for his spectacular swerving free-kicks.

GABRIEL BATISTUTA
(Argentina)

▶ **One of the many star South Americans,** known as *Batigoal* to fans. Back to his best after some disappointing games.

DAVID BECKHAM
(England)

◀ **Very young,** but he is a vital member of coach Hoddle's squad.

33

The World Cup is now the largest sporting event of all, bringing in huge sums in ticket sales and television fees. And the 16th competition will be by far the biggest of the lot. There are 32 nations taking part (eight more than four years ago), with 15 from Europe, five from South America, five from Africa, four from Asia and three from the North-Central American region. The programme involves 64 matches in 33 days, which requires a great deal of organisation.

FIFA general secretary Sepp Blatter makes the draw

Stade Velodrome, Marseille

The draw for the first round was staged at huge expense in Marseille last December. It was set up in such a way that the leading "seeded" nations were kept apart until the later stages, in the hope of providing the most exciting possible climax.

Football, of course, does not always run to plan...

JUNE 1998

Wednesday 10 June
FIRST ROUND
Brazil v Scotland
Morocco v Norway

Thursday 11 June
FIRST ROUND
Italy v Chile
Cameroon v Austria

Friday 12 June
FIRST ROUND
France v South Africa
Saudi Arabia v Denmark

Saturday 13 June
FIRST ROUND
Paraguay v Bulgaria
Spain v Nigeria
South Korea v Mexico
Netherlands v Belgium

Sunday 14 June
FIRST ROUND
Yugoslavia v Iran
Argentina v Japan
Jamaica v Croatia

Monday 15 June
FIRST ROUND
England v Tunisia
Romania v Colombia
Germany v USA

Tuesday 16 June
FIRST ROUND
Brazil v Morocco
Scotland v Norway

Wednesday 17 June
FIRST ROUND
Chile v Austria
Italy v Cameroon

Thursday 18 June
FIRST ROUND
South Africa v Denmark
France v Saudi Arabia

Friday 19 June
FIRST ROUND
Nigeria v Bulgaria
Spain v Paraguay

Saturday 20 June
FIRST ROUND
Belgium v Mexico
Netherlands v South Korea

Sunday 21 June
FIRST ROUND
Argentina v Jamaica
Germany v Yugoslavia
USA v Iran

Monday 22 June
FIRST ROUND
Colombia v Tunisia
Romania v England

Tuesday 23 June
FIRST ROUND
Italy v Austria
Chile v Cameroon
Brazil v Norway
Scotland v Morocco

Wednesday 24 June
FIRST ROUND
France v Denmark
South Africa v Saudi Arabia
Spain v Bulgaria
Nigeria v Paraguay

Thursday 25 June
FIRST ROUND
Netherlands v Mexico
Belgium v South Korea
Germany v Iran
USA v Yugoslavia

Friday 26 June
FIRST ROUND
Argentina v Croatia
Japan v Jamaica
Romania v Tunisia
Colombia v England

Saturday 27 June
SECOND ROUND
Match 2 B winner v A second
Match 1 A winner v B second

Sunday 28 June
SECOND ROUND
Match 3 C winner v D second
Match 4 D winner v C second

Monday 29 June
SECOND ROUND
Match 6 F winner v E second
Match 5 E winner v F second

Tuesday 30 June
SECOND ROUND
Match 7 G winner v H second
Match 8 H winner v G second

JULY 1998

Friday 3 July
QUARTER-FINALS
Match a Match 1 winner v Match 4 winner
Match b Match 2 winner v Match 3 winner

Saturday 4 July
QUARTER-FINALS
Match c Match 5 winner v Match 8 winner
Match d Match 6 winner v Match 7 winner

Tuesday 7 July
SEMI-FINALS
Match a winner v Match c winner

Wednesday 8 July
SEMI-FINALS
Match b winner v Match d winner

Saturday 11 July
3rd/4th PLACE PLAY-OFF

Sunday 12 July
WORLD CUP FINAL

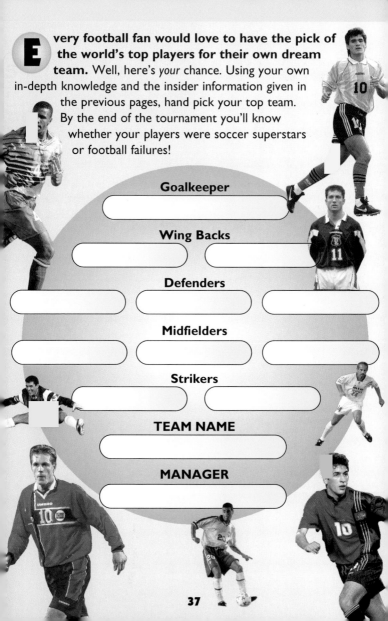

Every football fan would love to have the pick of the world's top players for their own dream team. Well, here's *your* chance. Using your own in-depth knowledge and the insider information given in the previous pages, hand pick your top team. By the end of the tournament you'll know whether your players were soccer superstars or football failures!

Goalkeeper

Wing Backs

Defenders

Midfielders

Strikers

TEAM NAME

MANAGER

GROUP A

Brazil
Scotland
Morocco
Norway

	Score		Score
Wednesday 10 June *St Denis, Paris*	Brazil ----> ◯	Scotland ----> ◯
Wednesday 10 June *La Mosson, Montpellier*	Morocco ----> ◯	Norway ----> ◯
Tuesday 16 June *Parc Lescure, Bordeaux*	Scotland ----> ◯	Norway ----> ◯
Tuesday 16 June *La Beaujoire, Nantes*	Brazil ----> ◯	Morocco ----> ◯
Tuesday 23 June *Velodrome, Marseille*	Brazil ----> ◯	Norway ----> ◯
Tuesday 23 June *Geoffrey Guichard, St Etienne*	Scotland ----> ◯	Morocco ----> ◯

When all the games have been played, fill in the table in the correct order
(3 points for a win; 1 point for a draw).

Team	Won	Drawn	Lost	Goals for	Goals against	Points
Enter 1A and 2A on page 46 in the second round						

1A

2A

GROUP B

**Italy
Chile
Cameroon
Austria**

Italian fans

		Score		Score
Thursday 11 June *Parc Lescure, Bordeaux*	Italy	◯	Chile	◯
Thursday 11 June *Municipal, Toulouse*	Cameroon	◯	Austria	◯
Wednesday 17 June *Geoffrey Guichard, St Etienne*	Chile	◯	Austria	◯
Wednesday 17 June *La Mosson, Montpellier*	Italy	◯	Cameroon	◯
Tuesday 23 June *St Denis, Paris*	Italy	◯	Austria	◯
Tuesday 23 June *La Beaujoire, Nantes*	Chile	◯	Cameroon	◯

When all the games have been played, fill in the table in the correct order
(3 points for a win; 1 point for a draw).

Team	Won	Drawn	Lost	Goals for	Goals against	Points	
							1B
							2B
Enter 1B and 2B on page 46 in the second round							

GROUP C

**France
South Africa
Saudi Arabia
Denmark**

Danish fans

		Score		Score
Friday 12 June *Felix Bollaert, Lens*	Saudi Arabia	○	Denmark	○
Friday 12 June *Velodrome, Marseille*	France	○	South Africa	○
Thursday 18 June *Municipal, Toulouse*	South Africa	○	Denmark	○
Thursday 18 June *St Denis, Paris*	France	○	Saudi Arabia	○
Wednesday 24 June *Gerland, Lyon*	France	○	Denmark	○
Wednesday 24 June *Parc Lescure, Bordeaux*	South Africa	○	Saudi Arabia	○

When all the games have been played, fill in the table in the correct order
(3 points for a win; 1 point for a draw).

Team	Won	Drawn	Lost	Goals for	Goals against	Points
Enter 1C and 2C on page 46 in the second round						

1C

2C

GROUP D

Spain
Nigeria
Paraguay
Bulgaria

Municipal, Toulouse

Score **Score**

Friday 12 June
La Mosson, Montpellier
Paraguay ----▶ ◯   Bulgaria ----▶ ◯

Saturday 13 June
La Beaujoire, Nantes
Spain ----▶ ◯   Nigeria ----▶ ◯

Friday 19 June
Geoffrey Guichard, St Etienne
Spain ----▶ ◯   Paraguay ----▶ ◯

Friday 19 June
Parc des Princes, Paris
Nigeria ----▶ ◯   Bulgaria ----▶ ◯

Wednesday 24 June
Felix Bollaert, Lens
Spain ----▶ ◯   Bulgaria ----▶ ◯

Wednesday 24 June
Municipal, Toulouse
Nigeria ----▶ ◯   Paraguay ----▶ ◯

When all the games have been played, fill in the table in the correct order
(3 points for a win; 1 point for a draw).

Team	Won	Drawn	Lost	Goals for	Goals against	Points
Enter 1D and 2D on page 46 in the second round							

1D

2D

GROUP E

**Netherlands
Belgium
South Korea
Mexico**

St Denis, Paris

		Score		Score

Saturday 13 June
Gerland, Lyon
South Korea → ◯ Mexico ----→ ◯

Saturday 13 June
St Denis, Paris
Netherlands → ◯ Belgium ----→ ◯

Saturday 20 June
Parc Lescure, Bordeaux
Belgium ----→ ◯ Mexico ----→ ◯

Saturday 20 June
Velodrome, Marseille
Netherlands → ◯ South Korea → ◯

Thursday 25 June
Geoffrey Guichard, St Etienne
Netherlands –→ ◯ Mexico ----→ ◯

Thursday 25 June
Parc des Princes, Paris
Belgium ----→ ◯ South Korea –→ ◯

When all the games have been played, fill in the table in the correct order
(3 points for a win; 1 point for a draw).

Team	Won	Drawn	Lost	Goals for	Goals against	Points	
							1E
							2E
Enter 1E and 2E on page 47 in the second round							

GROUP F

Germany
USA
Yugoslavia
Iran

American fans

		Score		Score

Sunday 14 June *Geoffrey Guichard, St Etienne*	Yugoslavia →	◯	Iran ----→	◯
Monday 15 June *Parc des Princes, Paris*	Germany ---→	◯	USA ----→	◯
Sunday 21 June *Felix Bollaert, Lens*	Germany ---→	◯	Yugoslavia →	◯
Sunday 21 June *Gerland, Lyon*	USA ----→	◯	Iran ----→	◯
Thursday 25 June *La Mosson, Montpellier*	Germany ---→	◯	Iran ----→	◯
Thursday 25 June *La Beaujoire, Nantes*	USA ----→	◯	Yugoslavia →	◯

When all the games have been played, fill in the table in the correct order
(3 points for a win; 1 point for a draw).

Team	Won	Drawn	Lost	Goals for	Goals against	Points	
							1F
							2F
Enter 1F and 2F on page 47 in the second round							

43

GROUP G

**Romania
Colombia
England
Tunisia**

(English fan)

		Score		Score

Monday 15 June *Velodrome, Marseille*	England ---→ ◯	Tunisia ---→ ◯
Monday 15 June *Gerland, Lyon*	Romania ---→ ◯	Colombia ---→ ◯
Monday 22 June *La Mosson, Montpellier*	Colombia ---→ ◯	Tunisia ---→ ◯
Monday 22 June *Municipal, Toulouse*	Romania ---→ ◯	England ---→ ◯
Friday 26 June *St Denis, Paris*	Romania ---→ ◯	Tunisia ---→ ◯
Friday 26 June *Felix Bollaert, Lens*	Colombia ---→ ◯	England ---→ ◯

When all the games have been played, fill in the table in the correct order
(3 points for a win; 1 point for a draw).

Team	Won	Drawn	Lost	Goals for	Goals against	Points	
							1G
							2G
Enter 1G and 2G on page 47 in the second round							

44

GROUP H

**Argentina
Japan
Jamaica
Croatia**

| Gerland, Lyon |

Score   **Score**

Sunday 14 June
Municipal, Toulouse   Argentina --→ ◯   Japan ----→ ◯

Sunday 14 June
Felix Bollaert, Lens   Jamaica ----→ ◯   Croatia ---→ ◯

Saturday 20 June
La Beaujoire, Nantes   Japan ----→ ◯   Croatia ---→ ◯

Sunday 21 June
Parc des Princes, Paris Argentina --→ ◯   Jamaica ---→ ◯

Friday 26 June
Parc Lescure, Bordeaux   Argentina --→ ◯   Croatia ----→ ◯

Friday 26 June
Gerland, Lyon   Japan ----→ ◯   Jamaica ----→ ◯

When all the games have been played, fill in the table in the correct order
(3 points for a win; 1 point for a draw).

Team	Won	Drawn	Lost	Goals for	Goals against	Points
Enter 1H and 2H on page 47 in the second round						

1H

2H

45

Once the first round matches have been completed, enter the teams in the spaces below and record the results of the second round matches.

Match 1

1A

2B

Saturday 27 June
Parc des Princes, Paris
Enter the winners on line 1 in the quarter-finals on page 48.

Match 2

1B

2A

Saturday 27 June
Velodrome, Marseille
Enter the winners on line 2 in the quarter-finals on page 48.

Match 3

1C

2D

Sunday 28 June
Felix Bollaert, Lens
Enter the winners on line 3 in the quarter-finals on page 48.

Match 4

1D

2C

Sunday 28 June
St Denis, Paris
Enter the winners on line 4 in the quarter-finals on page 48.

Felix Bollaert, Lens

Match 5

1E → 2F →

Monday 29 June
Municipal, Toulouse
Enter the winners on line 5 in the quarter-finals on page 48.

Match 6

1F → 2E →

Monday 29 June
La Mosson, Montpellier
Enter the winners on line 6 in the quarter-finals on page 48.

Match 7

1G → 2H →

Tuesday 30 June
Parc Lescure, Bordeaux
Enter the winners on line 7 in the quarter-finals on page 48.

Match 8

1H → 2G →

Tuesday 30 June
Geoffrey Guichard, St Etienne
Enter the winners on line 8 in the quarter-finals on page 48.

La Mosson, Montpellier

Quarter-finals

Match a

1 → ◯   **4** → ◯

Friday 3 July
La Beaujoire, Nantes
Enter the winners on line a on page 49.

Match b

2 → ◯   **3** → ◯

Friday 3 July
St Denis, Paris
Enter the winners on line b on page 49.

Match c

5 → ◯   **8** → ◯

Saturday 4 July
Velodrome, Marseille
Enter the winners on line c on page 49.

Match d

6 → ◯   **7** → ◯

Saturday 4 July
Gerland, Lyon
Enter the winners on line d on page 49.

Team ( )

Substitutes

Goal scorers

World Cup Champions 1998

( )

Runners-up

( )

What do you know about the World Cup?

Try your luck at these 12 questions – the answers can all be found in this book. When you have answered all 12, take the first letter of the first word of each answer and arrange them so they spell the name of a man with a place in football history.

1 Italian father, Italian son

2 First name of England's top striker

3 Country whose team nickname is *Bafana Bafana*

4 Top scorer in the 1966 tournament

5 Country managed by a 'Brown' man

6 Top of the South American qualifiers

7 Player who missed the last penalty in the shoot-out in the 1994 Final

8 Country managed by Slobodan Santrac

9 He played in two World Cup Finals for two countries

10 Anghel is his first name: what is his second name?

11 Music popular with Jamaican players?

12 Country that hosted the Final 60 years ago

Top player

At the end of the competition the official *Man of the Tournament* will be named. Who will it be? Make your choice here—before the first ball has been kicked!

The World Cup Final
France 1998
Sunday 12 July • St Denis, Paris

Team ⬭

Substitutes

Goal scorers